NEW ORLEANS

IN PHOTOGRAPHS

NEW ORLEANS

IN PHOTOGRAPHS

In collaboration with the travel experts at Fodor's

Sharon Keating

GRAMERCY BOOKS
NEW YORK

Credits
Editor: Anne McDowall
Designer: Axis Design
Picture Researcher: Rebecca Sodergren
Production: Kate Rogers
Reproduction: Anorax

Additional captions
Page 1: The riverboat "Natchez"
Page 2: Greek Revival-style house at 2265 St. Charles Avenue

Picture Acknowledgements

L=Left R=Right C=Center T=Top B= Bottom

© **Alamy Images:** © Geogphotos/Alamy 6. / © Andre
Jenny/Alamy: 76B, 114.
© **Chrysalis Image Library** 20T, 36-37, 49B, 54, 71, 75,
77, 78T, 105B, 117B.
© **Corbis:** 11 © Robert Holmes/CORBIS 2, 22, 51T, 61B,
85, 98T, 98B, 106-107, 108. / © Lee Snider/Photo
Images/CORBIS: 32-33. / © Richard Cummins/CORBIS 74. /
© William Manning/CORBIS: 86B. / © Philip Gould/CORBIS:
94T, 113, 116, 118-119. / © DAVID RAE
MORRIS/Reuters/Corbis:121.
© **Penny Tweedie / Getty Images:** 26-27.
© **Hotel Monteleone:** 49T.
© **Le Pavillion Hotel** / Ron Calamia 78B.
© **Lonely Planet Images** / Ray Laskowitz: 12B. / © Lonely
Planet Images / Richard Cummins: 28. / © Lonely Planet
Images / Michael Aw: 39. / © Lonely Planet Images /Thomas
Downs: 50. / © Lonely Planet Images /Lee Foster 56. / ©
Lonely Planet Images / Ray Laskowitz 76T. / © Lonely Planet
Images /Thomas Downs:124. / © Lonely Planet Images / Ray
Laskowitz: 125.
© **New Orleans Pharmacy Museum:** 52B.
© **Photolibrary.com:** 1, 7, 8-9, 12T, 13, 14-15, 17, 19, 20B,
24, 29, 30, 31T, 34, 40-41, 43, 44-45, 46, 53, 51B, 55T, 55B,
57, 59, 64B, 66,67, 68, 69, 81, 82-83, 86T, 91B, 92,103,
104, 115, 128.
© **Richard Gardner/Rex Features:** 61T, 117T.
© **Stanley Beck:** 18, 21, 23, 25, 31B, 35, 38, 42, 47, 48, 52T,
58, 60, 63, 64T, 65, 79, 84, 87, 88, 89, 90, 91T, 93, 94-95B, 96,
97, 99, 101, 102, 105T, 109, 110T, 110B, 111, 122, 123.
© **1992 Brantley & Brantley Photography:** 73.
© **Windsor Court Hotel:** 72.

Contents

INTRODUCTION

In 1699, two French brothers, Iberville and Bienville, proposed a city in a crescent-shaped bend in the Mississippi River in the Louisiana Territory. Seemingly uninhabitable by anything other than mosquitoes—and a place where even the Native Americans refused to live—the city remained just an idea until the French awarded a proprietorship to the Company of the West. The company, which was owned by John Law, appointed Jean Baptiste Le Moyne, Sieur de Bienville, Commandant and Director General of the new colony.

In 1718, Bienville's dream of a city became reality. From the beginning, the reason for New Orleans' existence was the mighty Mississippi, the main highway for trade with the New World. Bienville made friends with the Native American Choctaw Nation, who showed him a way to enter Lake Pontchartrain from the Gulf of Mexico and travel on to Bayou St. John to the site where the city now stands. This shortcut eliminated the need to navigate the extremely treacherous waters at the mouth of the river, and considerably shortened the route.

The city streets were laid out in 1721 by Adrian de Pauger, the royal engineer, following the design of Le Blond de la Tour. Many of the streets are named for the royal houses of France and Catholic saints. Contrary to popular belief, Bourbon Street is named not after the alcoholic beverage but rather after the Royal House of Bourbon, the family then occupying the throne in France.

Survival in the colony was difficult. The population of New Orleans constantly battled the forces of nature in the form of hurricanes and floods. Because New Orleans is below sea level and has a sub-tropical climate, the original wooden structures built directly on the ground soon decayed. The challenges presented by the geography forced the French to re-invent their methods of construction. They found

French Quarter Buildings: *The Vieux Carré, commonly called the French Quarter, is really as much Spanish as it is French. It is the Spanish who gave the area its wonderful lacy ironwork— so prominent in the Vieux Carré—when the city was rebuilt during Spanish rule after the two great fires of the 1700s.*

Mississippi River: *The Mississippi has always been the lifeblood of New Orleans. It is the reason New Orleans exists. The river, which drains 40 percent of all of America, is 200 feet deep at the Crescent City Connection Bridge and over a half mile wide.*

that native cypress woods defied rot and thick brick walls helped provide some insulation.

The city remained under French rule until 1763, when the colony was sold to Spain. Two major fires—in 1788 and 1794—destroyed much of the city and, consequently, the French architecture. The first fire started in the Chartres Street home of the Spanish treasurer Don Jose Nunez. Because it was Good Friday, a lit candle had been placed on the altar of the private chapel in the home. The candle ignited the altar cloths and the fire quickly spread throughout the home. The priests had padded the church bells on this holy day, preventing the warning from going out, and the flames quickly engulfed the city. By the time the fire was over, a vast majority of New Orleans had been destroyed. Only the Ursuline Convent and a row of houses along the levee were left standing. The city began to be rebuild, but in 1794, children playing on Royal Street accidentally set fire to a hay store and again the citizens awoke to destruction. After the second fire, the Spanish decreed new building ordinances requiring tile roofs and native brick walls.

Late in the eighteenth century, a revolt of the free people of color and slaves in Saint-Domingue (Haiti) brought a number of refugees and immigrants to Louisiana. These people added to the cultural mix of New Orleans. They were skilled artisans and well educated and made their mark in politics and business. One such successful newcomer was James Pitot, who later became the first mayor of incorporated New Orleans.

Because of its history, the Vieux Carré, or, as it is more commonly known, the French Quarter, actually has more Spanish influence in its architecture than French. For example, St. Louis Cathedral is French in design, but the Cabildo abutting it was the Spanish seat of government. The "lacy" iron balconies that abound in the Vieux Carré are a Spanish legacy. New Orleans thrived under the rule of the Spanish until 1803, when the Louisiana Territory was ceded back to the French. The French-speaking population rejoiced—until France almost immediately sold the territory to the Americans.

The Creoles—the first generation born in the new world—were of French and Spanish origin and considered themselves superior to the Americans. By the time of the Louisiana Purchase in 1803, New

Orleans had become a cosmopolitan city with an established society. The only contact the Creoles had with Americans was with the rowdy flat-boatmen who came down the Mississippi River to trade. The Creoles made no secret of their disdain for the Americans and refused to associate with them socially. The Creoles went further and insisted the Americans live on the upriver edge of the city. The two areas were divided by a commons, now

Canal Street (so named because of an unrealized canal). The median was a neutral ground. That tradition still persists in New Orleans, which has "neutral grounds", not medians, on every divided street. The division makes navigation in the city difficult because no street name is continued from the French Quarter into the American Sector. For example, Royal Street on the downriver side of Canal Street is St. Charles Avenue on the other side.

Jackson Square: *This square is the heart of the Vieux Carré. It is a beautifully landscaped public area, which is at the center of life for New Orleanians and visitors alike. It is bordered by the St. Louis Cathedral, the Cabildo, and the Presbytère.*

New Orleans was now a divided city. The Creoles coexisted with the free people of color in the Vieux Carré and the Americans began to build their own city upriver from Canal Street. In the new area, called Faubourg Ste. Marie, or the neighborhood of St. Mary, the Americans set up their own version of the Creole city. St. Patrick's Church became the new St. Louis Cathedral, Lafayette Square mimicked Jackson Square, and Gallier Hall, behind the square, was the seat of the American government. As time went on, the Creoles expanded downriver into Faubourg Marigny and toward Lake Pontchartrain into Treme. The Americans spread out upriver into the Livaudais Plantation that later became the Garden District.

In 1812 war broke out between the Americans and the British. The British, recognizing the strategic importance of the port of New Orleans, sought to take over the city. In the well-known Battle of New Orleans, General Andrew Jackson and his American forces teamed up with Jean Lafitte and his band of pirates to defeat the British at Chalmette, just south of the city. Although the battle was unnecessary because the war had actually ended before it took place, it was a great moment in New Orleans history. Credit for the victory was given to Our Lady of Prompt Succor, to whom the Ursuline nuns prayed during the battle and in whose honor a mass is still celebrated every January 8th.

By the 1840s, New Orleans had become the third largest and the wealthiest city in America. Several factors contributed to this success. Steamboats made travel to New Orleans a pleasant, less arduous journey and facilitated the import and export of cash crops and manufactured goods. People of all nationalities flocked to New Orleans as the city became a major international port. Cotton and sugar growers in the area became wealthy and New Orleans became the banking center of the country. Banking institutions lined Royal Street and businesses all over the country preferred currency from Louisiana banks because of their reputation for solvency. The "Dix", or ten-dollar bills, printed in French on one side and English on the other, was the currency of choice for commerce. "Dix" became "Dixie" and now refers to all things Southern.

The Civil War ended this period of prosperity. New Orleans surrendered early on and was occu-
pied by the Union Army throughout the war. Louisiana endured the longest period of reconstruction of any of the Southern States. Although decimated financially, New Orleans escaped the fate of Atlanta and was able to maintain the integrity of her architecture and culture.

At the close of the nineteenth century, the legal Red Light District, known as Storyville, gave birth to the uniquely American musical genre of Jazz.

By the dawn of the twentieth century, New Orleans began to emerge again as a major port filled with an amalgamation of people and cultures. She remains unique among American cities: not entirely American, Southern, Caribbean, or European, but a blend of all of these influences.

The "Big Easy", as New Orleans is known, has a reputation for tolerance of all cultures and beliefs. Voodoo is still practiced as a religion among the descendents of the Saint-Domingue immigrants, and Mardi Gras is celebrated in the French tradition. African-Americans developed their "tribes", known as the Mardi Gras Indians, who parade in their various neighborhoods. The Irish celebrate St. Patrick's Day alongside the Italians with their St. Joseph's Day activities. Jazz bands still process mournfully to the cemetery and dance the "second line" on the way home from a funeral. The growing Asian and Hispanic populations are developing new traditions that soon all New Orleanians will embrace.

Modern-day New Orleans is a celebration of life in a joyous combination of cultures, history, and people. She continues to hold her place as a center of commerce and a major tourist destination. In what other city can you find a Superdome filled with as many people cheering a voodoo priestess performing a cleansing ceremony before a Saints game on one Sunday afternoon as are praying with the Pope on another? New Orleans is not simply a city to visit, she is an experience not to be missed!

▶ **Mardi Gras Indians:** *One of the many traditions of Mardi Gras is the Mardi Gras Indians. These groups of mainly African-Americans began marching more than a century ago in their inner-city neighborhoods and have kept up the tradition. They formed tribes, rather than the better-known, mostly white krewes and adorned themselves with beautiful, handmade costumes. Each wonderfully beaded costume takes more than one year to make.*

◁ **Cemetery at Sunset:** *The practice of above-ground burials in New Orleans is partially cultural and partially for climatic reasons. The heritage of the French founders of the city combined with the impracticality of burying underground in a city that is below sea level make for many "Cities of the Dead" in New Orleans.*

▷ **Jazz Bands:** *Jazz emerged from the parlors of the houses of Storyville presided over by such madams as Josie Arlington. It was refined and made famous by Jelly Roll Morton, Buddy Bolden, Louis Armstrong and others. New Orleans continues to express herself in her native "tongue."*

◁ **Voodoo Rituals:** *The Voodoo in New Orleans is a legitimate religious practice, not that of the evil spells and zombies presented by Hollywood. Voodoo priestesses perform the rites of Voodoo before the altars for various needs and positive purposes and vestiges of such practices are often seen around town.*

▷ ▷ **Downtown:** *The skyline of New Orleans is a contrast of old and new. Skyscrapers are a recent development in New Orleans because the technology to construct tall buildings on land that is so swampy was not perfected until the 1960s.*

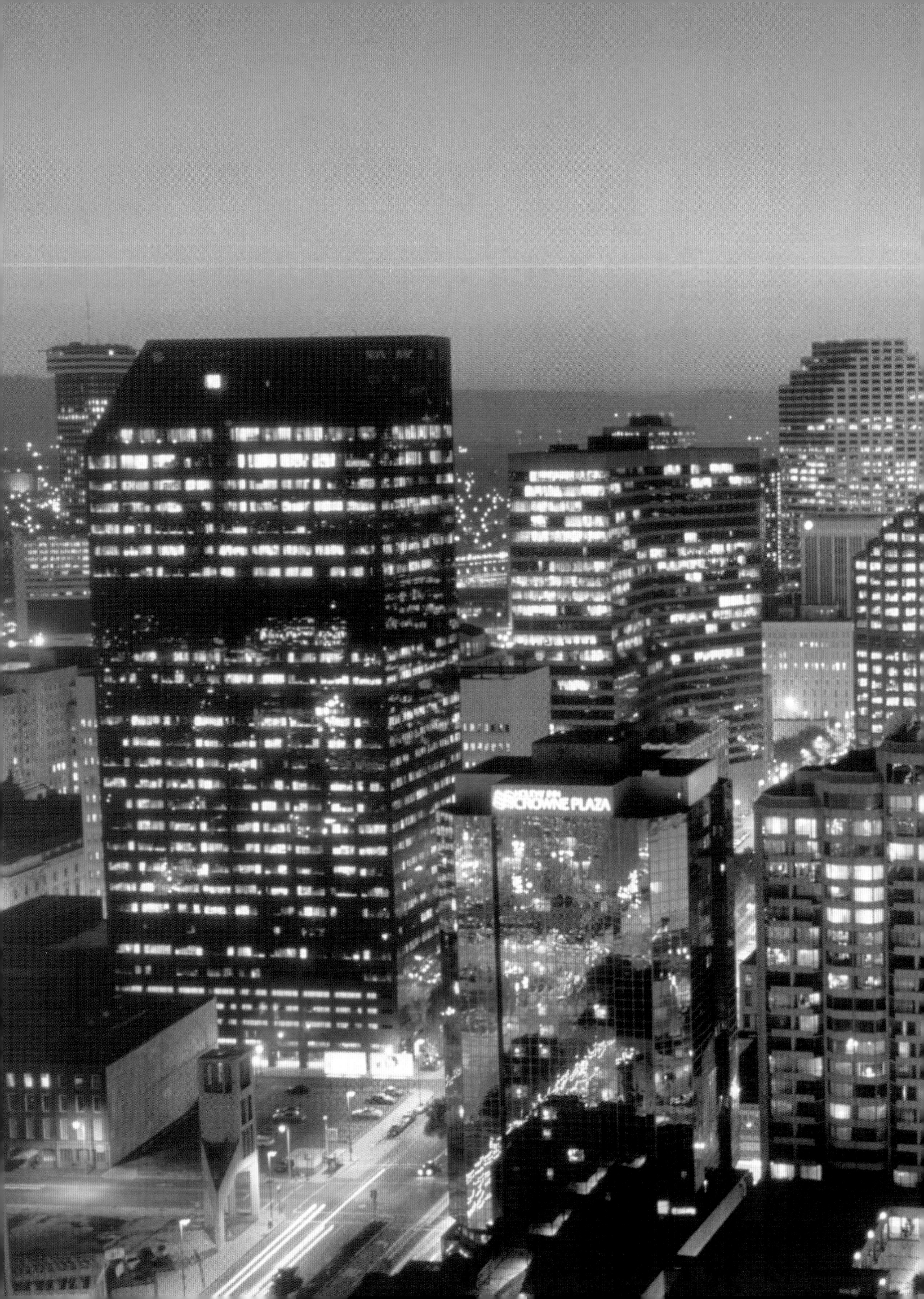
CROWNE PLAZA

French Quarter

The oldest area of the city, commonly called the French Quarter, is more properly known as the Vieux Carré because although it was founded by the French, it reflects the art and architecture of the Spanish era as well. In the late nineteenth century it became unfashionable and fell into disrepair. Many of its now-elegant buildings had become little better than slums. In the mid-twentieth century, historic preservationists who recognized its irreplaceable value successfully launched the rehabilitation and authentic restoration of this eighteenth-century "time capsule."

The French Quarter is bounded by Rampart Street, Esplanade Avenue, Canal Street, and the Mississippi River. Within its confines there are several distinct neighborhoods. The most well-known area is, of course, the entertainment section, with its numerous restaurants, bars, and hotels. Eateries are as varied as the Lucky Dog vendor and the fine Creole dining of Arnaud's or Galatoire's. Music emanates from the clubs on Bourbon Street, Preservation Hall, and the House of Blues—and, for that matter, from nearly any street corner on any given day. Mementoes from the past can be purchased in the many antique shops on Royal Street. A walk down Decatur Street culminates at the bustling Old French Market, where the Indians traded long before Bienville arrived. Quiet streets and old Creole cottages in the lower quarter contrast with the raucous party of the popular tourist destinations.

Along the edge of the quarter, the "Ladies in Red," the newer streetcars, traverse the streets on the banks of the Mississippi. Beyond the floodwalls, which are necessary to save the city from catastrophic flooding, is the green expanse of Woldenberg Park. Constructed atop old wharves, the Park provides a relaxing place to view the activities on the busy river, where modern tankers and cruise ships sail alongside paddle-wheeled steamboats. Here, the beauty of the Crescent that attracted Bienville is easy to recognize. The cacophony of sounds is amazing here—the calliope on the steamboat "Natchez", the plaintive sounds of a lone trumpeter on the Moonwalk, the lusty singing of street performers all fill the air with a sense of excitement.

At the heart of the French Quarter is Jackson Square, flanked on two sides by the famed Pontalba Apartments and, at its top, by the St. Louis Cathedral, the Cabildo, and the Presbytère. The square is the scene of constant activity: artists display their paintings, while tarot-card readers tell the future, and all the while dancers, performance artists, mimes, musicians, and clowns celebrate the multicultural flavor of the city. Mules boasting jaunty straw hats pull open carriages for those who prefer their sightseeing at a more leisurely pace.

At the edge of the upper quarter, Canal Street demonstrates the contrast between the Creole sector (Vieux Carré) and the American sector on the other side. Double signs indicate that the old French "Rues" end at Canal Street and the "new" American streets begin on the other side. Between the two sectors runs the widest main street in all of America.

Rampart Street is the inner boundary of the Vieux Carré. This was the edge of the original city and the place where New Orleans buried the throngs of those who were lost to the yellow-fever epidemics of the early years of the city.

Although the city of New Orleans has expanded on all sides, its heart remains the French Quarter.

▶ **Horse-drawn Carriage:** *There's no better way to enjoy the sights and sounds of the Vieux Carré than by taking a ride in one of the carriages that travel through the area—a relaxing respite in a world that sometimes moves too fast.*

▲ **Exchange Alley:** *In the 1800s, this alley, now the site of restaurants and art galleries, was the main street of commerce and was considered out-of-bounds for women. It was also the center for dueling masters and Creoles would send their sons to learn the art of dueling here.*

▶ **Jackson Square:** *This beautifully landscaped public space, overlooked by St. Louis Cathedral, is the heart of the Vieux Carré and at the center of life for New Orleanians and visitors alike. When Adrian de Pauger laid out the city in 1721, he put a parade ground in this spot and it has remained a public square ever since. It was renamed Jackson Square in 1856 by the Spanish Baroness Michaela Almonester Pontalba.*

◀ **The Cabildo:** *This building became the seat of Spanish government in 1763 and of the entire Mississippi Valley in the late 1800s. The Cabildo has witnessed many historic events, including the signing of the Louisiana Purchase in 1803. These days, with the neighboring Presbytère, it serves as the Louisiana State Museum. The death mask of Napoleon Bonaparte is displayed prominently in the Cabildo.*

▶ **Pirate's Alley:** *Running between St. Louis Cathedral and the Cabildo, this alley is still paved with the original stones used as ballast on ships sailing down the Mississippi River in the early days of the city. Although the origin of the alley's name is unknown, it is generally thought to be named for Jean Lafitte, a buccaneer and smuggler who helped General Andrew Jackson defeat the British in the Battle of New Orleans during the war of 1812.*

◀ **The Presbytère:** *Built in 1724, the Presbytère is one of the two historical buildings flanking the St. Louis Cathedral. The building was originally a monastery and home to one of New Orleans' best-loved Spanish Capuchin priests, Father Antonio de Sedella, after whom the alley between the Presbytère and the Cathedral is named. The Presbytère is now part of the Louisiana State Museum.*

▲ **Pontalba Apartments:**

Among the oldest apartment
buildings in the U.S., these
grand rowhouses were erected
in the 1850s by Michaela
Almonester Pontalba. Today
they house stores on the
lower level and apartments
on the upper levels, as was
the Creole tradition.

▶ **Galatoire's
Restaurant:** Serving fine
Creole food since 1905,
Galatoire's is one of New
Orleans' premier restaurants.
Lunch at Galatoire's the
Friday before Mardi Gras is a
longstanding tradition among

New Orleanians. Because
the restaurant does not
take reservations, lines form
outside the day before and
many college students earn
money by sleeping in line
to hold places for more
affluent diners.

◁ **Antoine's Restaurant:** *This renowned New Orleans restaurant was opened in 1840 by Antoine Alciatore and has remained in family hands ever since. Antoine created one of New Orleans' favorite dishes, Oysters Rockefeller, so named for the richness of the sauce. Antoine's maintains the quality with which it began, and over the years has seen many famous and infamous diners .*

▶ **Tujague's:** *Tujague's has been a New Orleans landmark since 1856 when Madame Begue's first served her "petite dejeuner" (brunch) in the Creole tradition. Inside the Paris-style bistro is a beautiful cypress bar that survived Prohibition.*

▶ ▶ **Old French Market:** *New Orleanians have come to this market for food for more than 200 years. Even before the French arrived, the Indians used this spot for trading. The current stalls and arcades were constructed between 1813 and 1822, and remodeled in the 1930s. Today, farmers and fishermen from all over southern Louisiana come daily to sell their produce and catches. At the Esplanade Street end of market is a flea market with varied and interesting items for sale.*

◀ **Bienville Statue:**
Jean Baptiste le Moyne, Sieur de Bienville, founded New Orleans in 1718 and named it for the king's brother, Louis Philippe, Duke of Orleans. His statue stands on Decatur Street.

▶ **Joan of Arc Statue:**
Joan of Arc, the Maid of Orleans, is the patron saint of the city of New Orleans. This statue was a gift from the people of France to the people of New Orleans in 1959 and is an exact replica of the statue in Orleans, France. It now stands in the Place de France near the entrance to the Old French Market on Decatur Street.

Armstrong Park:
A statue of Louis Armstrong, one of New Orleans' favorite sons, stands in this beautiful park filled with grassy knolls and lagoons. The park sits at the edge of the French Quarter and is connected to Congo Square and the Mahalia Jackson Performing Arts Center.

Faulkner House Books: *William Faulkner lived in this unassuming house in Pirate's Alley and wrote his first book, A Soldier's Pay, here. The building now houses a small bookstore bearing Faulkner's name. The Pirate's Alley Faulkner Society, also based here, supports and promotes Southern writers.*

Lalaurie House:
This elegant three-story Vieux Carré mansion was the site of the worst crime in New Orleans history. Delphine Macarty LaLaurie and her husband Dr. Louis Lalaurie, who bought the house in 1832, enjoyed a high place among the Creoles until a fire broke out on the night of April 10, 1834. Firemen found many slaves chained to the walls in the attic, the victims of horrible torture and mutilation. Word spread quickly and a lynch mob formed, but the Lalauries escaped. The house is reputedly haunted.

◀ **Brennan's Restaurant:** *This venerable restaurant is a breakfast must when visiting New Orleans. It is housed in a building constructed in 1795 after the last great fire of New Orleans destroyed the original building. During the course of its existence, the building has served as a private home, and the home of the first financial institution in the Louisiana Territory, the Banque de la Louisiane.*

◀ **Preservation Hall:**

In the rustic, authentic space
of Preservation Hall, dedicated
to keeping New Orleans Jazz
music alive, the sounds of real
New Orleans music played
by the best of New Orleans
artists is heard nightly.

▲ **Beauregard-Keyes
House:** This house, built in
1826, has had several famous
occupants. Paul Morphy, the
famous American chess
player was born here; B.G.T.
Beauregard, the Confederate
general, lived in the house for

a short time; Frances
Parkinson Keyes lived and
wrote several of her best-
selling novels here. It was
she who restored the house
and the surrounding gardens,
both of which are now open
for public tours.

▶ **Ursuline Convent:**
*This is one of the two oldest
buildings in New Orleans,
having survived the great
fires of 1766 and 1788. The
Ursuline nuns came to New
Orleans in 1727 and soon
began to teach those who
would not be educated under
the French and Spanish rule.
The building served as a
school for girls and Indians,
and also housed the residence
of the archbishop and
was a meeting place for
the Louisiana Legislature.*

 **Madame John's Legacy:** *Originally three structures—the main residence, a separate kitchen to prevent the spread of fire to the main house, and a garconnière, for the young boys of the household—the house is an excellent example of Louisiana Creole residential design at the end of the eighteenth century. Madame John's is now on the register of historic places and exhibits the work of local artists.*

▶ **Jackson Brewery:** *Once an active brewery for a favorite local beer, the Jackson Brewery is now filled with restaurants, shops, and condos. In its heyday the Jackson Brewery was the largest independent brew house in the South and the tenth largest in the country. It has been a famous landmark in New Orleans since its construction in 1891.*

Pat O'Brien's: *In a city of bars, Pat O'Brien's is the joint. Whether you're sitting in the courtyard or in the piano bar, the air is filled with music and fun. One of the famous New Orleans drinks, the Hurricane, was invented here.*

 **St. Anthony's Garden:** *This lovely garden situated behind St. Louis Cathedral is a pleasant area that was the site of many duels in the early days of New Orleans. For the Creoles, dueling was a sport used for settling disputes and they dueled only to first blood. When the Americans came into the city after the Louisiana Purchase, the sport changed to a deadly business and it was later banned from the garden.*

▶ **St. Louis Cathedral:** *This beautiful cathedral was preceded by a humble wood-and-brick church built by the original settlers in the 1720s. The cathedral is named for St. Louis, who ruled France as Louis X. It was destroyed by fire in 1788 and was rebuilt between 1792 and 1794 with money donated by Don Andres Almonaster y Roxas, who is buried under the altar.*

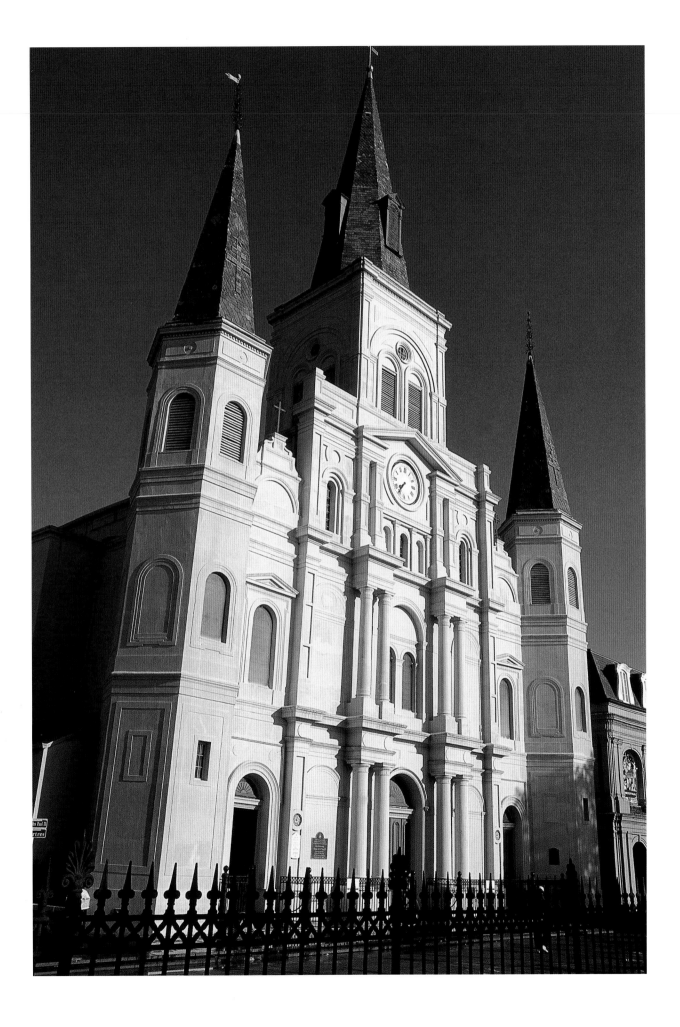

▶ **Royal Street:** *A stroll down Royal Street today, with its antique shops and fine restaurants, is a delightful experience. In the 1800s it was a street of commerce and banking. The streetcar named Desire ran on tracks down Royal Street and it was on this street that an apothecary named Peychoud concocted a beverage of bitters and brandy and served it in an eggcup—coquetier in French. The Americans, who could not pronounce the French word, called the drink a "cocktail," thus originating the name.*

▲ **The U.S. Mint:** *At the edge of the Vieux Carré on Esplanade Avenue stands the old mint. This neo-classical structure was built by the United States Government in 1835 to mint coins and was in service until 1910. It is the only mint in the U.S. that minted both Union and Confederate coins. The building was turned over to the State of Louisiana and is now used as a museum.*

▶ **Bottom of the Cup Tearoom:** *Stop for a cup of tea and have your fortune read here. It all makes for a pleasant respite. But in the 1870s a "mixed-blood" mistress of a wealthy Frenchman fled her lover's bed one cold December night after an argument. Her nude and frozen body was found the next morning on the roof. Her ghost is seen in the building on cold nights.*

Muriel's Restaurant:
Prior to the Civil War, slaves
brought into the port of New
Orleans were kept here until
they were auctioned on the
slave block nearby. This may
account for the stories about
glasses flying off the bar and
crashing into the wall at this
famous restaurant. One ghost
believed to reside here is that
of Pierre Antoine Lepardi
Jourdan, who committed
suicide on the second floor
when he lost the house in a
poker game in 1814.

Hotel Monteleone:
This elegant hotel was
founded by Antonio
Monteleone, a cobbler from
Sicily who came to New
Orleans in the 1880s. The
hotel is still in family hands
and has undergone several
renovations in its history. It
remains one of the most
elegant in the Vieux Carré.

Old Absinthe House:
The building originally housed
an import business started by
two Spaniards in 1803. The
current name was adopted
in 1874 when a mixologist
created a drink of the same
name. Legend holds that Jean
Lafitte the privateer often
frequented the bar and
planned his attack on the
British here in the war of 1812.

◄ **House of Blues:**
A favorite venue for hearing live music in the French Quarter. The Gospel Sunday brunch features the best of Gospel music to feed the soul and a buffet to feed the body. The battle cry here on Sunday is "praise the Lord and pass the biscuits."

▶ **Lafitte's Blacksmith Shop:** *Lafitte's is one of the few remaining examples of early French architecture in New Orleans. Built sometime before 1772, it survived two major fires that destroyed most of the city. Legend has it that the Lafitte brothers, including Jean Lafitte, operated a blacksmith shop out of the building as a front for their privateer exploits. Today it is a favorite bar for locals and tourists alike.*

▶ **Bourbon Street:**
The best-known street in the Vieux Carré, Bourbon Street, or Rue Bourbon, is the location of many bars and nightclubs. Crowds flock to Bourbon Street clubs and spill over into the street nightly, but probably few of the revelers know that the street is named for the Royal House of Bourbon, not for the beverage many are drinking.

◀ Pharmacy Museum:
Located in the 1823 Creole townhouse of Louis J. Dufilho Jr., who became America's first licensed pharmacist in 1816, the Pharmacy Museum houses two floors of exhibits showing the history of healthcare and an herb garden in the courtyard.

▲ Historic French Market Inn: The beauty of the courtyard in this small inn is much of its charm. It was built in the 1800s by the Baron Joseph Xavier de Pontalba as a residence. The architecture is typical Creole, with the building at the edge of the property surrounding a private courtyard.

▶ Arnaud's Restaurant:
Arnaud's was founded in 1918 by a colorful French wine salesman named Arnaud Cazenave. "Count Arnaud" believed that a meal should be a celebration, a joy not to be missed, and this attitude toward food continues to prevail in New Orleans. When the Count died, his daughter Germaine Cazenave Wells took over the restaurant. Many say that both still inhabit it.

◀ **The Napoleon House:** *This house, also known as the Girod House, was constructed in 1814 by Nicholas Girod, the first elected mayor of New Orleans. Its current name has its root in a legend that holds that the Creoles in New Orleans were certain Napoleon would seek refuge here after his exile. Today the Napoleon House bar is listed by Esquire magazine as one of the 100 best bars in America.*

▶ **Creole Cottage:** *This small cottage is typical of Creole architecture. The façade abuts the banquette (sidewalk) and there are four bays, or openings, with solid shutters. The cottage also has a private courtyard in the back. The Creoles also built two-story townhouses in the Vieux Carré that had living quarters on the top and businesses on the bottom level and a courtyard in the rear.*

▶ **St. Jude's Shrine:** *St. Jude, the saint of the impossible, has a great presence in New Orleans. This international shrine is housed in the oldest church building in the city. Built in 1823 as a funeral chapel on the edge of town for the burial of yellow-fever victims, the chapel is now known as the Chapel of Our Lady of Guadalupe. Many come to the shrine to make a novena for the grant of an "impossible" favor.*

◀ **Hermann-Grima House:** *Built in 1831, this home has one of the most beautiful courtyards in the Vieux Carré and an American Colonial look that is unusual for French Quarter architecture. In 1924 it was acquired by the Christian Women's Exchange, which operated a shop and secure housing for women and children in need. It is now restored and open to the public for tours.*

▶ **Gallier House Museum:** *The renowned architect James Gallier, Jr., built this two-story townhouse in 1857. Now open to the public, it is beautifully furnished with period furniture and one of the city's earliest working indoor bathrooms.*

◀ **Brulatour Patio:**
The Creoles considered their
garden as private a space
as the bath, so it was always
walled and opened only to
the family. Walking past a

Creole townhouse or cottage
would not give a hint of the
lush garden beyond. The
Brulatour Patio is typical of
courtyards in the Vieux Carré.

▲ **Cornstalk Fence
Hotel:** Judge François Xavier-
Martin, first Chief Justice of
the Louisiana Supreme Court
and author of the first history
of Louisiana, lived in this
elegant Victorian home in

the 1800s. Today it is a small
hotel surrounded by a 165-
year-old, intricately designed
and beautifully painted
cast-iron fence, which gives
the hotel its name.

▶ **1850 House:** *One of the Pontalba buildings, which flank Jackson Square, the 1850 House is a period house museum furnished and decorated to reflect the mid-nineteenth-century lifestyle. It is owned and operated by the Louisiana State Museum.*

◀ **Historic New Orleans Collection:** *General Kemper Williams and his wife, Leila Moore, founded the Historic New Orleans Collection with the donation of their significant collection of papers and maps. The building contains reading and research rooms, and is a valuable source of information about New Orleans history.*

▶ **Voodoo Museum:** *Housing some of the artifacts of the practice of Voodoo in New Orleans, including Voodoo Queen, Marie Laveau's "wishing stump," which was believed to bestow blessings on those who touched it, the museum also seeks to correct some of the distorted images of the practice of Voodoo.*

Mississippi River

New Orleans has always drawn breath from the Mississippi River. The city began its life in 1718 on the banks of a large crescent in the Mississippi and has rested there comfortably ever since. The river is responsible for the diverse population and blend of cultures of present-day New Orleans.

In the early days of the city, boats traveling down its waters from ports north were not capable of traveling upstream, so the boats were disassembled and wood and ballast stones left on the banks of the river as the traders began their travel back home on foot. This provided the citizens of the Vieux Carré with lumber for construction of homes and stones for street-paving—a boon to a city below sea level with no natural stone. Trade on the Mississippi River also made the city rich in the middle of the nineteenth century after the Louisiana Purchase brought in trade from all over the world.

Today, this great river is not only a major highway of trade and commerce, it is also a place to relax, to board a steamboat for a ride back in history, or to hear the plaintive wail of a lone saxophone on a foggy day. Now, as in 1718, New Orleanians flock to the Mississippi River.

Woldenberg Park runs along the river at the edge of the Vieux Carré and was constructed atop old wharfs. It provides green space for city dwellers and a place to hear music, watch the river traffic, or just meditate. The Aquarium of the Americas and the Entergy IMAX® Theater in Woldenberg Park provide family entertainment. Every year in April, Woldenberg Park plays a big part in the French Quarter Festival. The park has two stages for music and is the venue for one of the two large Jazz brunches set up for the festival. At the edge of the park dock several paddle-wheelers, including the "Natchez" with its calliope playing and the "John James Audubon", which waits to take families upriver to the Audubon Zoo.

The Spanish Plaza, at the river in front of the Riverwalk Marketplace, is the site of the annual Lundi Gras celebration, when the kings of the Krewes of Rex and Zulu meet with great pomp and ceremony. The fountain in the Spanish Plaza is a favorite meeting place for friends before shopping at the Riverwalk, or going for an evening out in the Vieux Carré. New Orleans has become a major port of call for cruise ships and a walk along the Riverwalk often provides a view of several large cruise ships.

The Mississippi River is in the heart of every New Orleanian. It is even the basis for giving directions. Because New Orleans is in a crescent of the river, directions relative to compass points make no sense. There's no north, south, east or west. There's up or down, relating to the flow of the river. Whether you're a shopper, a music lover, or just want to take a walk beside one of the world's great rivers, the banks of the Mississippi River in the "Crescent City" are an enjoyable place to be.

▶ **Immigrant Monument:** *This graceful monument stands by the Mississippi River in Woldenberg Park as a tribute to many people from all over the world who immigrated to New Orleans. The Italians, Germans, Irish, French, Spanish, as well as those who came for South America and Africa, have all helped to shape the unique culture of New Orleans and are honored in this monument.*

◄ **Holocaust Survivors' Monument:** *Another of the monuments to be found while strolling through Woldenberg Park, this one remembers all those who were lost in the holocaust. Its circular design surrounded by benches encourages one to linger in reverence.*

◀ **Crescent City Connection:** *This bridge spans the Mississippi River at the foot of Canal Street in New Orleans. At this point the river, which drains 40 per cent of all of America, is 200 feet deep and more than a half mile wide. From the time Bienville founded the city in the "beautiful crescent" of the river in 1718 until the present, New Orleans has remained one of the most significant ports in the New World.*

▲ **Moonwalk:** *Behind Artillery Park and the Jackson Brewery, steps lead down to the water's edge. Named for former Mayor Maurice (Moon) Landrieu, the Moonwalk is a favorite place for visitors and locals to spend time as close to the river as you can get. There are usually solo trumpet players here and sounds and sights can be mesmerizing.*

◀ **"Ocean Song" Sculpture, Woldenberg Park:** *This large kinetic sculpture, near the statue of Woldenberg, was created by local artist John T. Scott. Built over former wharfs, the park follows the Mississippi River from the Moonwalk behind Artillery Park in the Vieux Carré to Canal Street. A stroll through the park offers views of the river and it's traffic, as steamboats, cruise ships, and container vessels travel up and down the river.*

▲ **Aquarium of the Americas:** *The world-class aquarium located on the river at the foot of Canal Street has more than one million gallons of fresh and saltwater exhibits spotlighting more than 430 species in fantastic habitats. It contains one of the largest and most diverse collections of sharks in the world. One favorite with children is the touch pool, where you can actually pet sharks and other exotic underwater creatures.*

◀ **Mississippi River Steamboats:** *Since its invention, the steamboat has been a part of the scene along the Mississippi River at the port of New Orleans. Today, steamboats such as the "Natchez", shown here, serve the port and are available for cruises of varying lengths and purposes. All offer a peek at what life was like on the Mississippi River in the nineteenth century.*

▼ **Spanish Plaza Fountain:** *At the foot of Canal Street, in front of the Riverwalk Marketplace, is an open plaza paved with Spanish tiles—a gift to New Orleans from Spain. The beautiful fountain in the center of the Spanish Plaza celebrates Spain's history in the New World and New Orleans. The fountain is lit at night and is often used as a backdrop for weddings.*

American Sector

A visitor to New Orleans must do two things—see the Vieux Carré and take the streetcar in the area of town known as the American sector.

The French were angry and rebellious when Louisiana was sold to Spain, an event that spawned several tragic uprisings. The Spanish newcomers were equally as proud and every bit as snobbish as their French neighbors. However, once the territory was sold to the U.S., these Creoles were unified with one common belief: that the rough-and-tumble Americans must be segregated from their cultured company. Canal Street became a kind of dividing line or commons area where the Creoles would conduct business with the Americans. The legacy of the separation of the Creoles and the Americans is still evident today on Canal Street: every street that crosses Canal from the Vieux Carré begins in the American sector with a new name.

The Creoles knew the Americans chiefly from the men who came downriver on flatboats for trade and commerce. These roughshod types were not typical of the Americans who came to settle in New Orleans—the businessmen and entrepreneurs who became rich from cotton and sugar, banking, and trade of every kind. The plantation upriver of Canal Street became the Faubourg Ste. Marie, or as the Americans who began to settle there called it, St. Mary. James Gallier designed and built Gallier Hall to rival the seat of government in the "Old Town." Lafayette Square was the American version of Jackson Square. St. Patrick's Church was constructed for the Irish immigrants and other Catholics who felt left out at St. Louis Cathedral. The Americans may not have had the pedigree of the Creoles, but they usually had a lot more money. The American sector is still home to the central business district of New Orleans. The main thoroughfare for business and commerce in the city is Poydras Street, which runs roughly parallel to Canal Street.

In the Faubourg Ste. Marie is a row of townhouses uncharacteristic of the general local architecture. Julia Row was built in the American Federal style with which northeasterners were comfortable. However, the weather and natural features of the city were at odds with these houses, which were built for a colder, drier climate and lacked the open galleries that allowed for air circulation. The residents used the first floor for part of their living quarters, but soon discovered that the periodic flooding required raised housing. These beautiful townhouses fell into disrepair, but have, in recent years, been restored to become the epicenter of the Arts District in New Orleans.

▶ **Gallier Hall:** *Dedicated in 1853, the Old City Hall is one of the finest examples of Greek Revival architecture in the U.S. Named in honor of its architect, James Gallier, Sr., it is the site of the grandstand from which the Mayor greets the Kings and Queens of Carnival during Mardi Gras.*

◀ **Windsor Court Hotel:** *Consistently ranked one of the top hotels in the U.S., the European-inspired Windsor Court has original paintings by Gainsborough and other artists of the last 400 years, afternoon Royal Tea, and museum-quality antiques. It is also home to the famous Grill Room.*

▲ **St. Patrick's Church:** *The Irish population in the American sector perceived discrimination at St. Louis Cathedral, which was dominated largely by the Creoles. In 1840, this Gothic church, with its 185-foot-high tower, was their splendid response. It is a now a National Historic Landmark.*

◄ **The National D-Day**
Museum: *The D-Day*
Museum is located on
Andrew Higgins Drive, named
for the New Orleans builder
who designed and
manufactured the landing
craft used in the invasions.
Founded by Dr. Stephen
Ambrose, it features artifacts,
films, oral histories, aircraft,
weapons, and uniforms. The
nearby Contemporary Arts
Center is a mecca for
alternative art forms.

▲ **Harrah's Casino:**
The only land-based casino
in the state, Harrah's
contains 115,000 square
feet of Las Vegas-style slot
machines, game tables, food,
and entertainment. At the
foot of Canal Street and
the Mississippi River, it is
now the site of John Besh's
Steakhouse. It seems New
Orleanians cannot do
anything without great food.

▲ **Louisiana Superdome:** *Completed in 1975 in the midst of the downtown business district, the Superdome expands over 52 acres, rises 273 feet into the skyline, and boasts the world's largest steel-constructed room without posts. It is the home of the New Orleans Saints' and Tulane University's football teams, and is also the venue for numerous concerts and shows.*

▶ **Lee Circle:** *This area was designated as Place du Tivoli and envisioned as the location for a children's merry-go-round in a proposed center of classical culture. The area was never developed, and after General Robert E. Lee died, the city donated the Circle as the site for his monument. General Lee stands with his arms crossed, defiantly facing the North.*

 **Fairmont Hotel:**

Formerly the Roosevelt Hotel,
the Fairmont was built in
1893. Here is possibly the
most beautiful hotel lobby
in New Orleans, especially
at Christmas, when it is
magically turned into a winter
fairyland, the Angel Hair
Lobby. The Sazerac Bar was
a favorite watering hole for
Huey P. Long.

◁ **Canal Street:** *This was a "commons" between the dignified Creole section (the French Quarter) and the new (rowdy) American sector. The canal proposed here was never built, and this street— the widest business-district street in the country—is the home today of hotels, businesses, and restaurants at one end, and of the famed cemeteries at its other.*

▷ **Louisiana Children's Museum:** *Located in a restored warehouse in the Arts District is the Louisiana Children's Museum, which features Mr. Bones, who shows the human skeleton in motion, and the Plasma Ball, which teaches light patterns. The museum's hands-on philosophy makes learning child's play: a child can pilot a boat down the Mississippi, step into a giant eyeball, or be a chef or a news anchor.*

◁ **Le Pavillion Hotel:** *Built in 1907, this completely restored "Belle of New Orleans" in the Central Business District houses stunning crystal chandeliers and antiques, and exudes Old World charm. The 20-foot Italian statues at the front door are "Peace" and "Prosperity." Le Pavillion is also reputed to be one of the most haunted hotels in the city.*

Uptown

Uptown is a directional term as well as a neighborhood one. In a city that hugs the serpentine curves of the Mississippi River, and is divided by culture at Canal Street, uptown means two things: it's upriver from Canal Street and it's generally past the statue of General Robert E. Lee. Uptown encompasses many neighborhoods, including the Garden District and the university area.

A great way to see all of uptown is on the St. Charles Avenue Streetcar, since St. Charles is the main street and passes through all of the smaller areas of uptown. The streetcar starts at Canal Street and travels upriver through the original American sector, and around Lee Circle, into the uptown area.

As the Americans moved upriver, they built grandiose mansions with large gardens on the subdivided Livaudais Plantation, now known familiarly as the Garden District. These homes of those wealthy merchants still impress today. Tours regularly stop at the mansion of Colonel Robert Short to admire the intricacy of the famous "Cornstalk Fence." Emile Commander established a restaurant catering to the area residents in the City of Lafayette; the City became part of New Orleans in 1852, and today this restaurant is the world-renowned Commander's Palace, a dining destination not to be missed. Across the street from Commander's is the Lafayette Cemetery, where movies requiring a graveyard scene are regularly filmed.

The beauty and elegance that is evoked by the name "Garden District" belies the origin of the name. When the Americans began to build these majestic homes, the Creoles were appalled and extremely critical. To a Creole, such an ostentatious display of wealth was proof that the Americans were without class. To put a garden in front for viewing by the public was tantamount to bathing in one's front yard. So, when the Creoles nicknamed the area the "Garden District," it was not complimentary.

The St. Charles Avenue Streetcar continues down the avenue for which it is named, and passes some of the most elaborate homes in the state. There is the "Wedding Cake" mansion, so-called because of its layers of intricate decoration on the façade; the Van Benthuysen-Elms Mansion, built in 1869 for Confederate officer Capt. Watson Van Benthuysen, a relative of Jefferson Davis; a replica of Tara; and the elegant Columns Hotel, to name just a few. Tulane and Loyola Universities are near the end of the Avenue, across from Audubon Park and the Audubon Zoo.

The streetcar ends at Carrollton Avenue, in the Old City of Carrollton, then turns around and begins its journey back. The visitor may choose to return to Canal Street via Magazine Street, which has become a European-flavored shopping destination with its shops, galleries, and cafés. This six-mile long "street of dreams," as it is called, runs through Audubon Park, Uptown, the Garden District, and the American sector.

▶ **Garden District:** *The area bounded by Jackson Avenue, Louisiana Avenue, St. Charles Avenue, and Magazine Street is where the wealthy Americans who came to New Orleans after the Louisiana Purchase eagerly sought to build their mansions. The rich soil was perfect for the colorful and elegant gardens that give this very exclusive area its name.*

▶ **Streetcars:** *The beloved Canal Street streetcars take the rider on a five-and-one-half-mile ride from the Old French Market to Mid-City. The St. Charles streetcar line is the oldest in the U.S., dating from 1835. It journeys 13 miles on St. Charles, from Canal Street to Carrollton Avenue, past some of the most beautiful mansions in the American sector. The green cars in current use were built in 1923.*

◀ **Columns Hotel:** *Built in 1833 and located at 3811 St. Charles Avenue, this hotel is on the National Register of Historic Places. Its impressive staircase and magnificent stained glass have provided a grand setting for many a movie filmed in New Orleans, and the Victorian Lounge has been voted one of the 100 best bars in America.*

▲ **Women's Opera Guild House:** *On Prytania Street in the Garden District, this house, furnished with period antiques, is a combination of Queen Anne and Greek Revival styles. Designed by William Freret and built in 1858 by a wealthy commission merchant, it was donated to the Women's Opera Guild in 1955.*

◁ **Audubon Park:**
Located on St. Charles Avenue across from Loyola and Tulane Universities, the park stretches out for 400 acres to the Mississippi River. Audubon Park was laid out by Fredrick Olmstead Law at the site of the 1894 World's Fair, and contains the Audubon Zoo. Ancient Spanish oaks, lagoons, green space, and gardens surround a new golf course.

▷ **Louise S. McGehee School:** *This is the Bradish Johnson House, built at 2343 Prytania Street around 1870. Designed by noted architect James Freret, who studied in Paris, the architecture is French Second Empire in style. It was formerly a private residence and is now a girl's school.*

◁ **Audubon Zoo:** *One of the premier zoos in the country is located in Audubon Park at 6500 Magazine Street. Along with elephants, primates, and jungle cats, the zoo features such exotic creatures as white alligators, white tigers (named Rex and Zulu), and Komodo dragons, as well as the Louisiana Swamp Exhibit.*

◄ **Van Benthuysen-Elms Mansion:** *This beautiful Italianate mansion on St. Charles Avenue was built in 1869 for Watson Van Benthuysen II, a Confederate Army Officer who became a wealthy businessman and the President of the St. Charles Streetcar company. The mansion's gazebo is a favorite destination for New Orleans weddings.*

▲ **Commander's Palace Restaurant:** *Located at 1408 Washington Avenue in the Garden District, Commander's Palace was established in 1880. It is considered one of the "Don't miss" dining experiences in New Orleans, serving splendid Creole and American food. The walls of glass in the Garden Room allow indoor diners to enjoy the beautiful patio.*

◀ **St. Alphonsus:** *This church was built by the Irish in 1855 on what is called the old "Ecclesiastical Square," across the street from the equally beautiful St. Mary's Church. It is now an Arts and Cultural Center, its restoration spearheaded by Anne Rice, one of New Orleans' most famous inhabitants.*

▶ **Tulane University:** *Named for Paul Tulane, who bequeathed more than one million dollars to endow a university, Tulane University, formerly the Medical College of Louisiana, was established as a private university in 1884. A law school was added later, then schools of liberal arts and sciences, and graduate studies.*

▶ **Loyola University:** *A private Jesuit university, Loyola is ranked among the top regional colleges and universities in the South and one of the top 60 in the U.S. Chartered as a university in 1912, it is located right next door to Tulane University at 6363 St. Charles Avenue.*

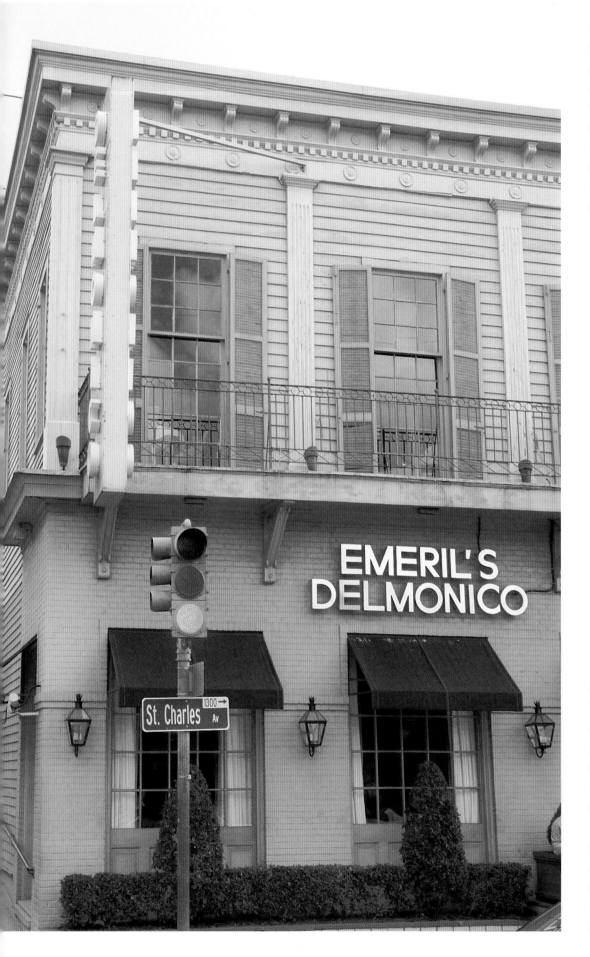

◀ **Delmonico's Restaurant:** *Delmonico's has operated as a restaurant since 1895 and was named after the steakhouse in New York. It is currently owned by the celebrated Emeril Lagasse, who serves his trademark Creole cuisine in its beautiful and very elegant interior.*

▶ **Tipitina's:** *The original Tipitina's, located at 501 Napoleon Avenue, was basically a neighborhood hangout where the colorful Professor Longhair, a musical legend, performed in the 1970s. Its stages are still the venue for countless local and internationally famous musicians in concert. "Tip's" has a recording studio and its own record label.*

Magazine Street:
Along Magazine Street, from
the central business district
to the river, is a six-mile array
of shops, restaurants, cafés,
antique shops, and galleries—

enough to satisfy the most
avid shopper. It is known
as the "Shopper's Street of
Dreams" and is easily
accessible by car or bus.

Coliseum Square:
Coliseum Square in the Lower
Garden District was the site
of a proposed Coliseum-like
stadium, in connection with
a classical arts school that

was never built. Today, the
park square is bordered by
beautiful homes such as
that formerly occupied by
Grace King, and is a popular
site for moviemakers.

◀ **Coliseum Theater:**
The Coliseum is located at Coliseum Square on the corner of Coliseum and Thalia streets. Built in the heyday of neighborhood movie shows, it closed in the early 1970s. Although the building was purchased and renovated on the exterior, maintaining as much of its old-time ambience as possible, it is not presently an active theater.

▶ **New Orleans Fire Department Museum:**
The Washington Avenue Firehouse, at 1135 Washington Avenue in the Garden District, was built in 1851. On view is an 1896 Steam Fire Engine, built especially for the city of New Orleans; a 1927 fire engine that could pump 750 gallons of water per minute; a collection of firemen's uniforms, and more.

◄ **St. Charles Avenue:**
*St. Charles Avenue runs
from the downtown central
business district to the
riverbend at Carrollton
Avenue. A ride on the St.
Charles Streetcar will reveal
this grand lady as she was
meant to be seen. Just past
Jackson Avenue, some of the
most beautiful mansions in
the city come into view. The
Avenue also boasts a diverse
collection of hotels, bars,
and restaurants.*

▶ **St. Elizabeth's
Orphanage:** *This lovely
building, at 1314 Napoleon
Avenue, was a refuge for
girls run by the Sisters of
Charity in 1871. Author Anne
Rice purchased it in 1992,
refurbishing it and making
it home to her extensive
antique doll collection, but
sold it in 2002, and it is
presently being converted
into luxury condominiums.*

◄ **Colonel Short's
Villa:** *The famous cornstalk
fence surrounds Colonel
Short's Villa at 1448 Fourth
Street in the Garden District.
This Italianate–Greek Revival
residence was built by
architect Henry Howard
in 1859. For a time, the
second occupational
governor during the Civil War,
Nathaniel Banks, made his
headquarters here.*

Mid-City and the Lakefront

Esplanade Avenue spans a portion of the city from the river to the City Park area. This street was the Creole version of St. Charles Avenue, and along the Avenue, on the Esplanade Ridge, are some of the most beautiful homes in the city, and some of the most historic. The Degas House at 2306 Esplanade is the only American home of Impressionist painter Edgar Degas and is now a lovely bed and breakfast. At the end of Esplanade is St. Louis Cemetery Number 3, which, along with the Lafayette Cemetery in the American Sector, is one of the most accessible and safest to visit.

At the end of Canal Street is the Cemeteries area of the City, where numerous burial grounds abut one another. Besides the more well-known, such as Metairie Cemetery and Greenwood, there is the "Odd Fellows Rest," the Masonic Cemetery.

The Bayou St. John neighborhood is a peaceful area along the Bayou itself, and includes the historic Pitot House at 1440 Moss St. City Park is accessible by the newly restored Canal Street streetcar, has an expanse of 1500 acres, and is home to the New Orleans Museum of Art, the New Orleans Botanical Garden, and the Besthoff Sculpture Garden. Several works by Mexican-born artist Enrique Alferez are placed throughout the park and its gardens. City Park has graceful lagoons for fishing and boating, and stately oaks where many a duel is rumored to have taken place. The antique wooden carousel in the Amusement Park is on the National Register of Historic Places and you can take a ride on one of two antique miniature trains.

Nearby is the historic New Orleans Fair Grounds, where New Orleanians have enjoyed thoroughbred racing since the mid-nineteenth century. The Fair Grounds also hosts the New Orleans Jazz Fest in April and May, a celebration of music and culture enjoyed by millions of people from all over the world.

The Lakefront area is mostly residential, and homes along the shores of Lake Pontchartrain are coveted for their view and beautiful, park-like surroundings. The University of New Orleans is situated here at one end of Lakeshore Drive, and the New Orleans Yacht Harbor more or less anchors the other end. The Mardi Gras Fountain with its musical dancing water is a beautiful night-light along the lakeshore. Spanning the lake is the Causeway, which, until recently, at 24 miles long, was the longest bridge over water in the world.

▶ **City Park:** *One of the largest urban parks in America, City Park contains 1,500 acres of lagoons, gardens, and mossy oaks. The park is also the home of the New Orleans Museum of Art.*

▲ **Pitot House:** *Located at 1440 Moss St., on Bayou St. John, this beautifully restored West Indies-style house was constructed in 1799 and was the home of James Pitot, sugar planter and first elected mayor of New Orleans. It is simple in design, as was typical of this style, and is only about a block from the streetcar line.*

▶ **City Park Rose Garden:** *Opened in 1936, this lovely sanctuary is an example of WPA public garden design from the Art Deco Period. The garden showcases not only the magnificent roses and other blooms, but also the work of Mexican artist Enrique Alferez. Today it is more commonly called the New Orleans Botanical Garden.*

◀ **Longvue Gardens:**

This Classic Revival-style house is set among eight acres of gardens and contains a wonderful collection of English and American antiques. It is located at 7 Bamboo Road. This was the home of Edgar and Edith Stern, extraordinary philanthropists and art collectors. The garden is in bloom with seasonal flowers throughout the year.

▶ **Bayou St. John:**

This was the route shown to Bienville by the Choctaws, permitting fairly safe passage from the Mississippi River to Lake Pontchartrain, and then to the Gulf of Mexico. Along the Bayou are homes from the Spanish Colonial period. This area is popular for fishing and casual boating.

▶ **City Park Lagoon:**

There are 11 miles of lagoons in City Park, which skirt a golf course and provide a beautiful setting for pedal boating and fishing—one resident caught a 22-pound catfish here. Swans, geese, and ducks share their home with sculptures from the Sculpture Garden.

◀ **"Dueling Oaks,"
City Park:** *The oaks in City Park are registered, and there is a map available with their various names and locations. There is one surviving "dueling oak," under which countless Creole gentlemen defended their honor to the death, despite laws forbidding such contests. These duels were usually fought with swords, although guns and other weapons were also used on occasion.*

◀ **New Orleans Museum of Art:** *This was formerly the Isaac Delgado Museum, built in 1911, and has a collection of more than 40,000 objects. It features works by Degas, Picasso, Miro, Renoir, and many others. The glass collection is one of the top five in the country, and on extended loan are exquisite Fabergé eggs.*

▶ **Ralph's on the Park:** *This is another restaurant from the peerless Brennan Family. Formerly a coffee house and concession stand for City Park, Ralph's, at 900 City Park Avenue, boasts a beautiful setting as well as the superb food for which the family is justly famous. A lovely dining balcony overlooks City Park.*

◄ **New Orleans Lakefront:** *Along the shores of Lake Pontchartrain are parks, exclusive neighborhoods, and universities. Families enjoy picnicking and fishing along the seawall of the second largest salt-water lake in the country.*

▶ **New Orleans Yacht Harbor:** *The municipal yacht harbor at West End Park on Lake Pontchartrain began as a project of the WPA in 1938. Countless boaters navigate crafts here, from sailboats to yachts.*

◄ **Causeway Bridge:** *The Lake Pontchartrain Causeway Bridge (actually twin spans) connects the south shore in New Orleans to the North Shore of the lake, and more than 30,000 cars a day travel over it. With an expanse of 24 miles, it was once the longest bridge in the world and is supported by 9,000 concrete pilings.*

Cities of the Dead

It is not contradictory to state that the Cities of the Dead, as New Orleans' cemeteries are called, are an integral part of life in the Crescent City. The early religious influences on the city are easily recognized in its capacity to honor the deceased. Yet beyond these influences is something more, something indefinable that seems to linger in the essence of all New Orleanians.

The above-ground vaults for which New Orleans is noted are as much a product of the topography as of the city's European and Caribbean pedigree. Because the city is entirely below sea level, the water tables are high, and frequent flooding, especially prior to the establishment of the protective levee system, made in-ground burials a dubious proposition. St. Peter's, the first city cemetery, was established in 1721, in the French Quarter, and utilized the customary below-ground burials. During rainy seasons, the caskets often became displaced.

In 1789, St. Louis Cemetery Number 1 was established, the first in the area with raised tombs. St. Louis Cemetery Number 2 was dedicated in 1823, followed by St. Louis Number 3 in 1854. The latter, along with Lafayette Cemetery in the Garden District, is one of the most easily accessible in the city. These cemeteries have tombs made of brick, and are usually plastered or whitewashed. The cemetery walls are surrounded by brick wall vaults that resemble old-style baker's ovens. These vaults save space by permitting multiple burials in small areas.

One of the more unusual cemeteries, even for New Orleans, is St. Roch's. Its chapel is most notable for the relic room, where plaster casts of body parts, braces, crutches, and the like, are placed in recognition of cures effected through the intercession of St. Roch. Praying for cures in a cemetery seems a bit curious to some people, but praying to find a husband, also a common practice at St. Roch's, may seem even more strange. The supplicants don't seem to think so, however.

A dramatic and fascinating type of burial is the "society tomb." In the nineteenth century, benevolent societies started to appear, and one of their functions was to erect large tombs for their members, who might otherwise not be able to afford a funeral. A large elk atop a mound in Greenwood Cemetery guards the remains of the members of the Order of Elks, while the Confederate Monument in Metairie Cemetery holds the remains of hundreds of Confederate soldiers.

On November 1—All Saints Day—New Orleanians pay special attention to their graveyards. Friends and relatives of the deceased turn out en masse, cleaning and painting tombs and decorating them with fall flowers and other mementoes. Religious services are held in the cemeteries. In early days, All Saints Day was quite a family event, when everyone socialized, bringing refreshments and leaving keepsakes. While this may seem bizarre to some, it is perfectly in keeping with the unusually strong spiritual soul of New Orleans.

▶ **St. Louis Cemetery Number 3:** *Established in 1854, this cemetery is the final resting place of Storyville photographer Ernest J. Bellocq and the restaurateur families of Prudhomme and Galatoire. The Byzantine tomb of the Hellenic Orthodox Community is an outstanding example of a "society" tomb—large tombs for members of designated groups, prominent here as in most New Orleans cemeteries.*

SCOTT – MARCHI
ERNESTINE SCOTT
M. C. GAIGNARD
NATALIE HALL SCOTT

▲ **Metairie Cemetery:**
Established on the site of the former Metairie Racecourse, this cemetery contains the most diverse architectural styles entombing a number of famous citizens. A sarcophagus denotes the tomb of Isaac Delgado, and Roman and Greek temples, an Egyptian pyramid, and a "bookshelf" can be seen among the many more traditional monuments.

▶ **Lafayette Cemetery Number 1:** *Originally the burial ground for the City of Lafayette, this is the site where most movies involving New Orleans' cemeteries are filmed. Some of the more poignant markers involve victims of the dreaded nineteenth-century yellow-fever epidemics and show several family members who died within days or hours of one another.*

◀ **Marie Laveau's Tomb:** *Marie Laveau was a free woman of color famous throughout Creole and black societies for her Voodoo practice. There is reason to believe that this is actually the tomb of her daughter, also named Marie, who was also a Voodoo practitioner. The elder Marie is believed to be buried in St. Louis Cemetery Number 2.*

▶ **St Roch's Cemetery:** *Established in thanksgiving by Father Peter Thevis after his congregation was spared during a yellow-fever epidemic, St. Roch's Cemetery is famous for its Good Friday Stations of the Cross and, somewhat oddly, its monuments to life as represented by a marble carving of a sick child who was cured.*

▶ **St. Louis Cemetery Number 1:** *Established in 1789, this is the oldest remaining cemetery in the city. Bounded by Basin, Conti, Treme, and St. Louis Streets, it is an active burial ground and contains the tombs of many notables, including chess master Paul Morphy, as well as the Glapion Tomb, where the remains of voodoo queen Marie Laveau are rumored to be buried.*

◀ **St. Louis Cemetery Number 2:** *This cemetery, consecrated in 1823, is separated from St. Louis Number 1 by the area of town formerly designated as "Storyville." It is the final resting place of (among many others) Jean Lafitte's lieutenant, the pirate Dominque You, and legendary rhythm & blues performer Ernie K-Doe, who is interred in the Twichell Family tomb.*

Festivals

New Orleans celebrates life! Numerous traditions and special days are rooted in the Catholic heritage of the city and celebrated in the style unique to New Orleans, with food, music, and festivities. Every New Year starts with a meal of cabbage and black-eye peas for luck and money, and the celebration of life begins.

Twelfth Night, or January 6, the day when the three wise men of the Bible visited the Christ Child, is referred to as "King's Day." The day marks the beginning of the Carnival season that will end on Mardi Gras Day, the day before Ash Wednesday. From King's Day to Mardi Gras, New Orleanians feast on King Cake and attend numerous balls and parades. On Mardi Gras Day, the whole city parties in the street until the stroke of midnight. At that time the authorities clear the streets and Ash Wednesday signals the beginning of Lent.

Two major holidays offer a chance to celebrate and break up the rigors of fasting for Lent. St. Patrick's Day on March 17 and St. Joseph's Day on 19 are celebrated by a week of festivities, which include parades and dances. St. Joseph's Altars in the many churches and homes of Italians are prepared, and open to the public in thanksgiving for relief from famine in Sicily in the Middle Ages. At the altars, New Orleanians, whether Italian or not, receive a fava bean that is supposed to bring them good luck throughout the year.

Easter Sunday marks the end of Lent and is celebrated by a parade through the Vieux Carré to the St. Louis Cathedral. This tradition was started by Germaine Cazenave Wells, the daughter of Count Arnaud, to show off her grand chapeaus. The Spring Fiesta, beginning on the first Friday after Easter, is a great time to see behind the façades of the grand homes of the Vieux Carré. Women of New Orleans, in ante-bellum dress, escort visitors on a candlelit tour of patios and courtyards not normally open to the public. Tours are also conducted in the Garden District and the Plantations on the river.

April is also a time to enjoy music and food at two big parties. The French Quarter Festival offers a variety of live music including Jazz, Classical, Rock, Cajun, and Zydeco in an outdoor setting. Stages are set up all over Woldenberg Park and the Vieux Carré. The world's largest Jazz Brunch is hosted in Jackson Square and Woldenberg Park with many local restaurants selling all types of food.

Soon after the French Quarter Festival, the city gears up for the New Orleans Jazz and Heritage Festival. This internationally known event takes place the last week of April and the first week of May. It is held at the Fair Grounds and is attended by hundreds of thousands of people who hear music greats from all over the world. As with any celebration in New Orleans, the food at Jazz Fest is abundant and legendary.

Fall brings the Swamp Fest at the Audubon Zoo, an event that brings New Orleans and her visitors out of doors after the hot, humid summer to enjoy the beautiful surrounds of Audubon Park. At Christmastime the Creole Revellion Dinners are offered at the fine Creole restaurants of the Vieux Carré, and Cajuns all along the Mississippi River light bonfires on the levee to light the path of Papa Noel. Finally, Christmas brings the faithful to St. Louis Cathedral in thankfulness for living in such a joyous place.

▶ **Mardi Gras Beads:** *If there is one universal symbol of Mardi Gras in New Orleans, it is Mardi Gras Beads. These are thrown from floats and balconies and everyone wears them during Carnival Season, even police officers. For months after Mardi Gras, beads are hanging from trees and telephone wires along the parade route, reminding everyone of the fun of the season.*

◄ **Mardi Gras Carnival**
Floats: *All Carnival parades*
have themes and, in all,
beads, cups, doubloons, and
other things are thrown to the
crowd from beautifully
decorated floats. There are
parades for more than two
weeks at Carnival time,
culminating on Mardi Gras
Day. Most parades in the city
travel the same route from
Uptown to Canal Street.

▲ **Mardi Gras Carnival**
Parade: *Carnival parades*
start on January 6 every year
and continue until Mardi Gras,
the day before Ash
Wednesday. The parades
are put on by private
organizations called "Krewes,"
who pay for the pageantry
from their own funds. Bands
and marching groups of every
description join in the fun.

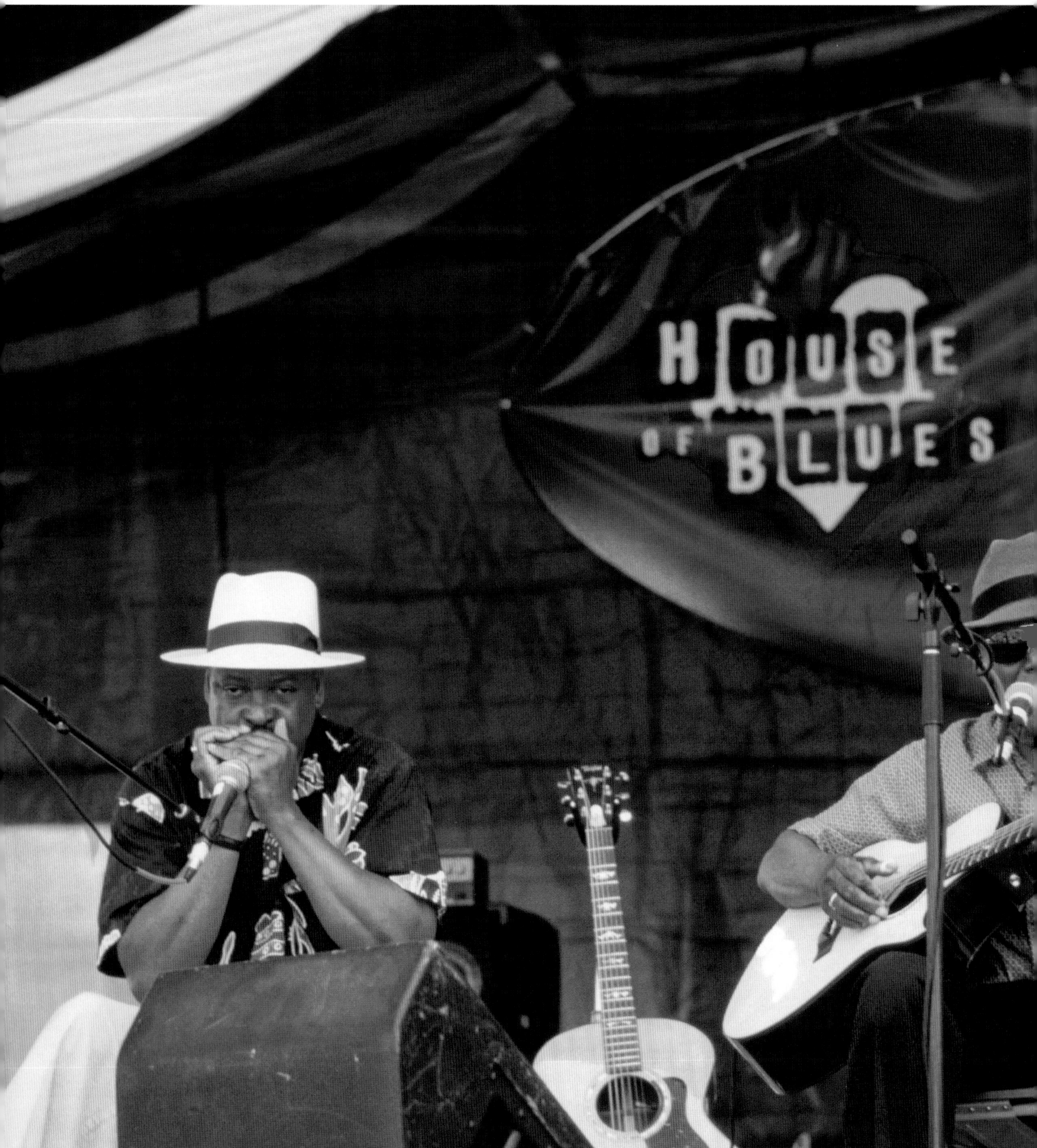
HOUSE
OF BLUES

◄ **New Orleans Jazz and Heritage Festival:** *The Jazz Fest, as it's known in New Orleans, is the city's second-largest celebration. Held the last weekend in April and the first one in May, Jazz Fest brings in hundreds of thousands of people each year to hear local, national, and international stars. The music is only half of the fun—the food is just as good!*

▲ **French Quarter Festival:** *Begun as a private party thrown by locals to get ready for Jazz Fest, the French Quarter Festival has now been discovered by the rest of the world and has turned into a mini Jazz Fest. Just like its big brother, the French Quarter Festival has great music and food—and it's free!*

Index

Map of New Orleans

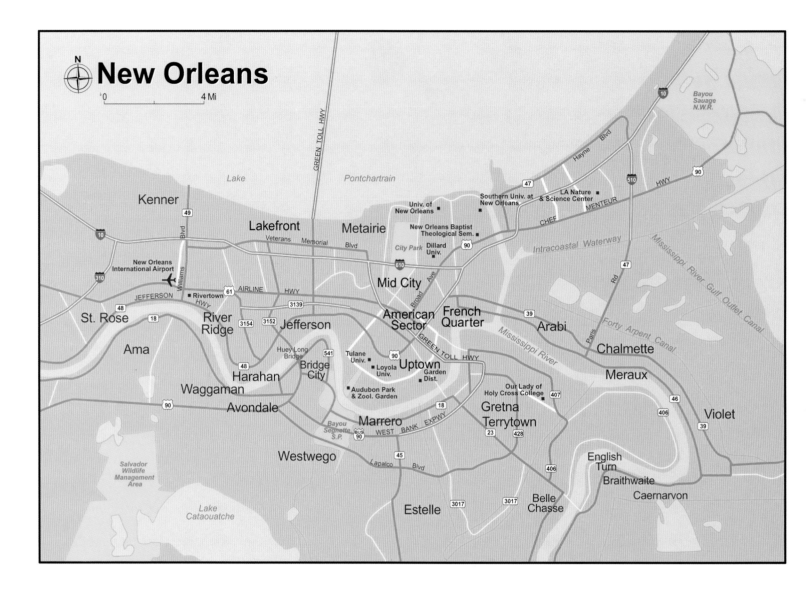